Hello!
I am a reindeer.

I0115149

Reindeer live in cold regions like the Arctic and subarctic.

Reindeer are also known as "caribou" in North America.

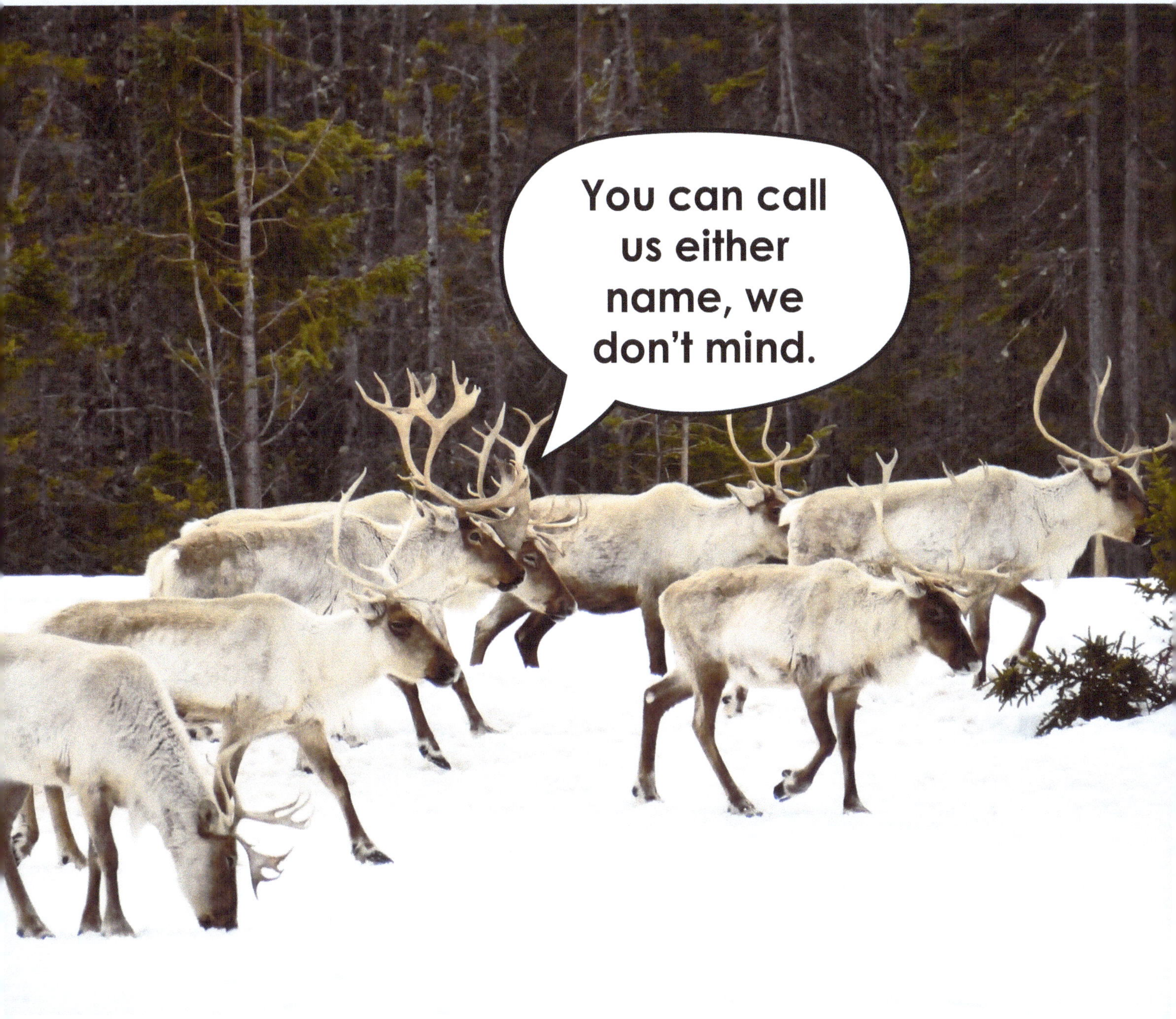

Reindeer have thick fur and hooves designed for snow.

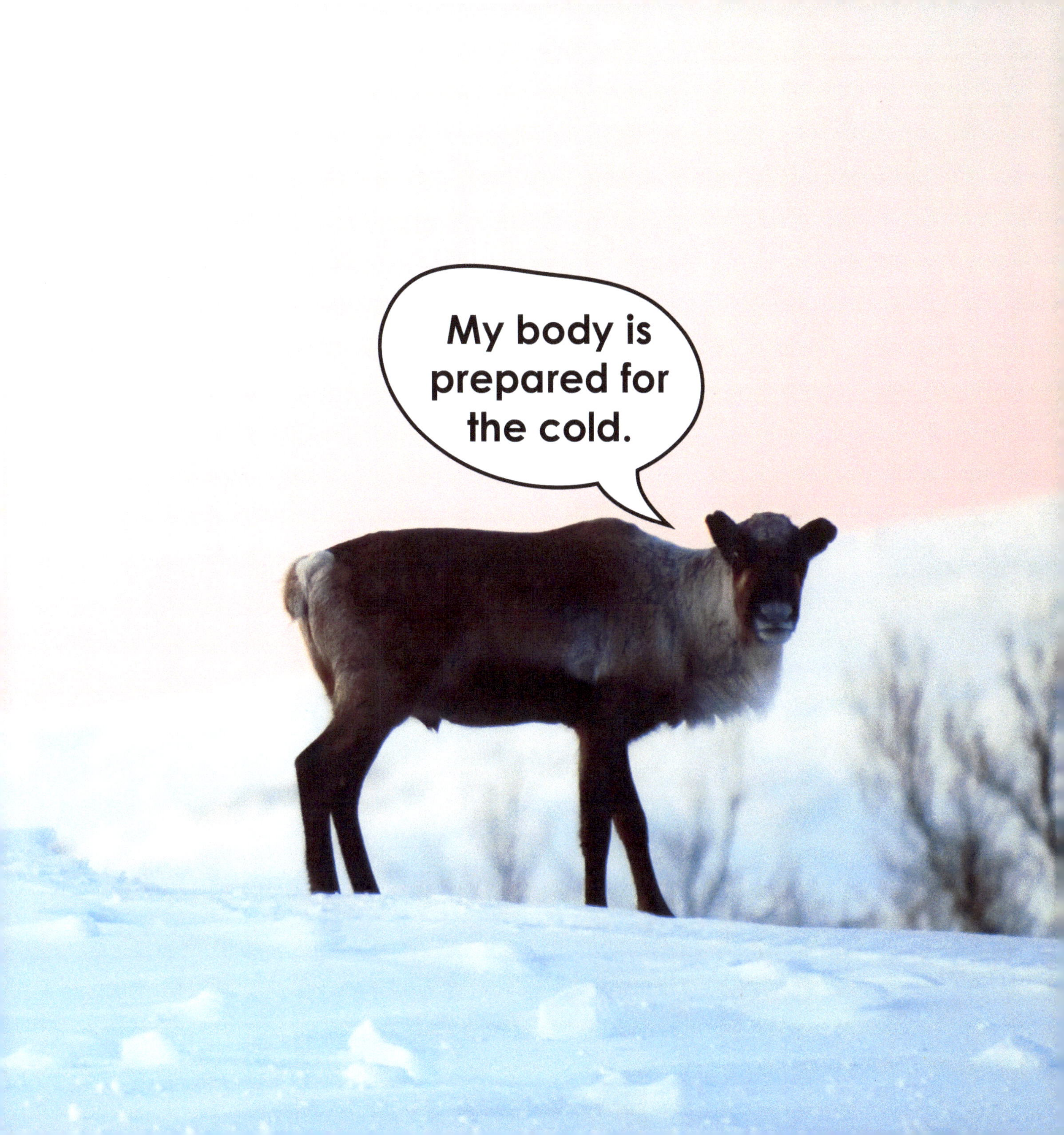
My body is prepared for the cold.

Reindeer fur changes color with the seasons.

My fur helps me blend into my environment.

Both male and female reindeer grow antlers...

...but the males' antlers are usually larger.

Antlers can be used for protection against predators.

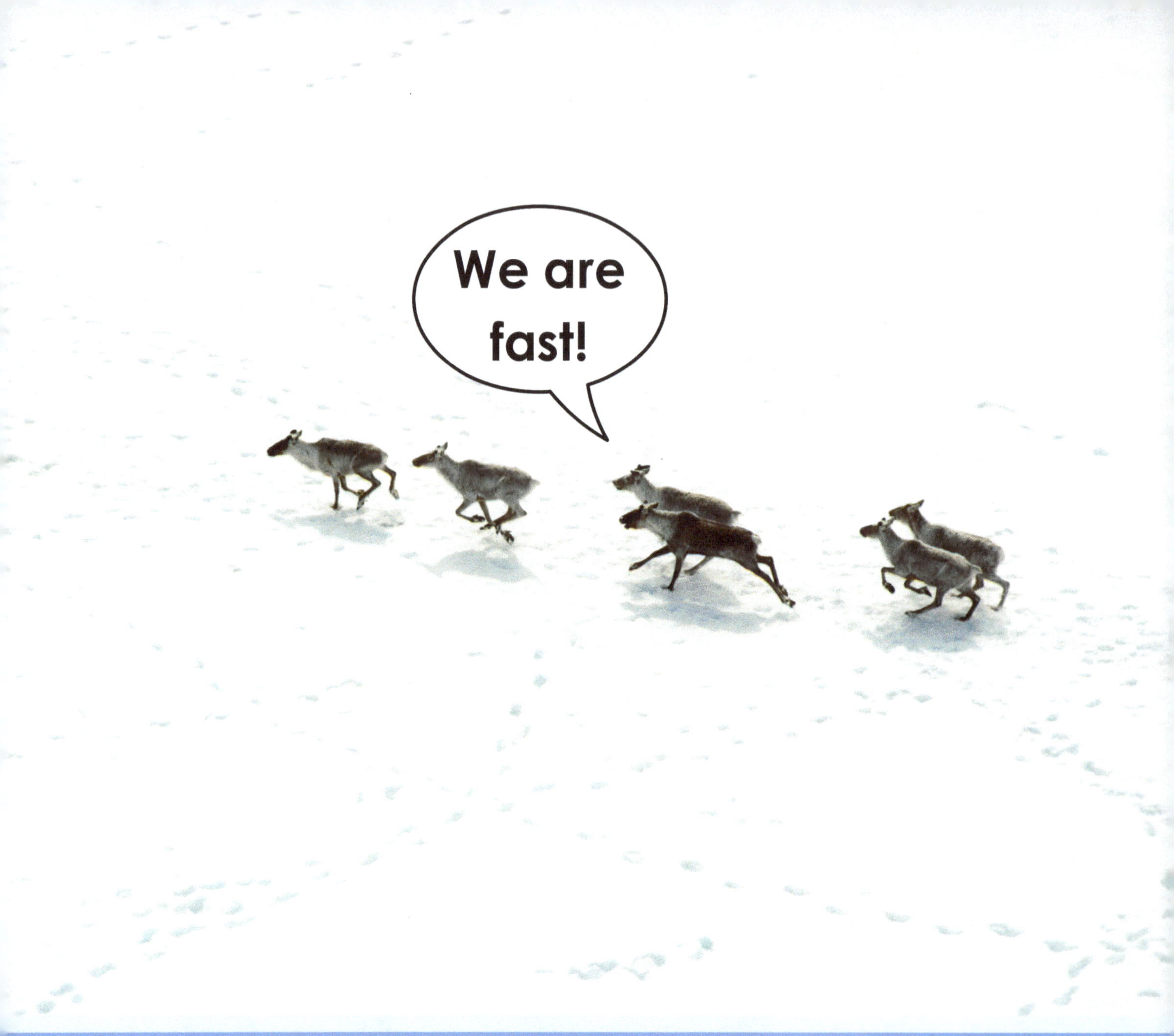

Reindeer can run at speeds of up to 50 miles (80 km) per hour.

Reindeer can travel up to 1,500 miles (2,414 km) or more in a year.

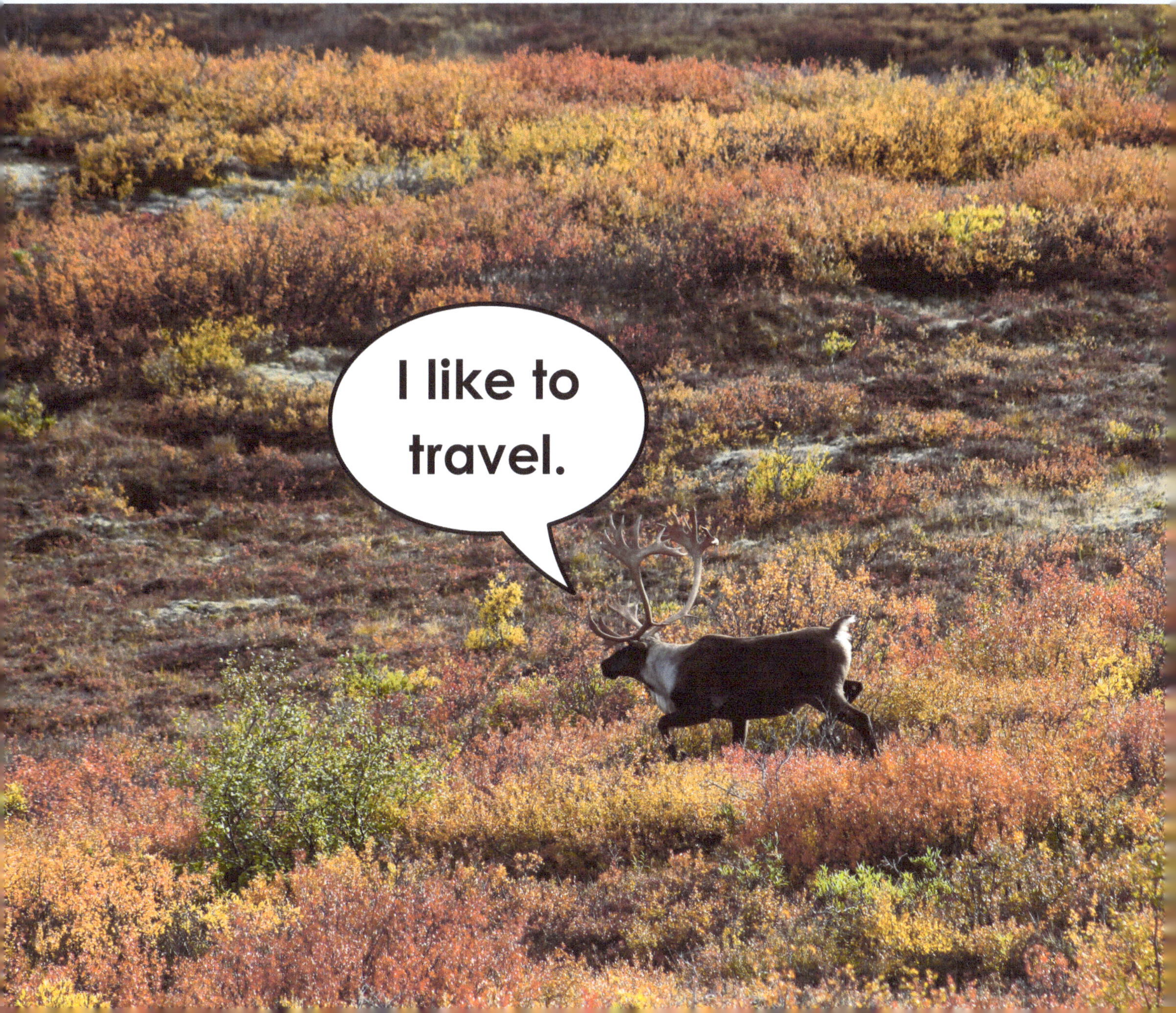

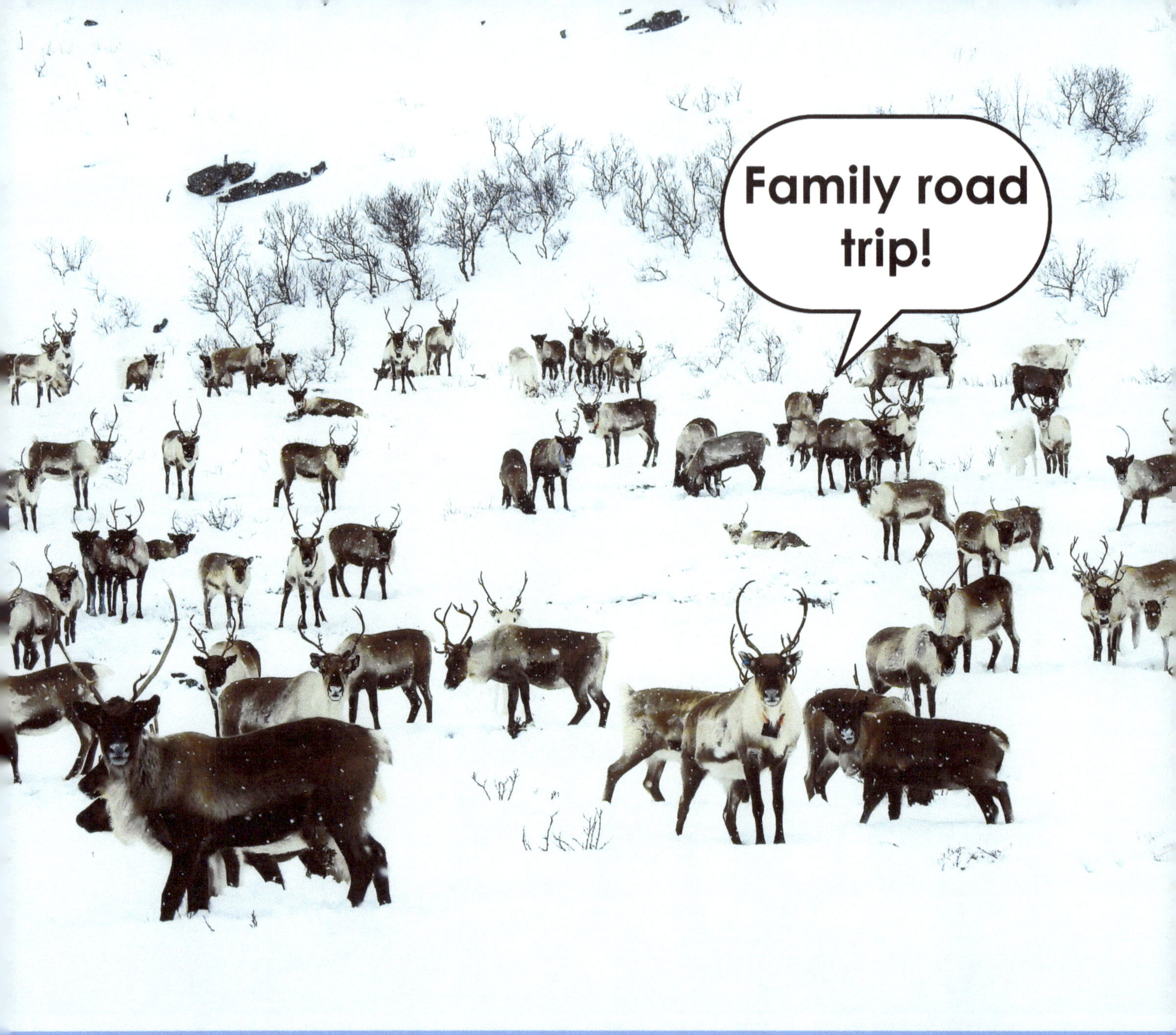

Reindeer are social animals and often travel in herds.

Reindeer herds can be as small as a few dozen or up to 200,000.

Reindeer communicate with each other using grunts and snorts.

When they are in a group, they stomp their hooves on the ground to make a soft drumming sound.

It's like our own secret language.

Reindeer have an excellent sense of smell, which helps them find food in the snow.

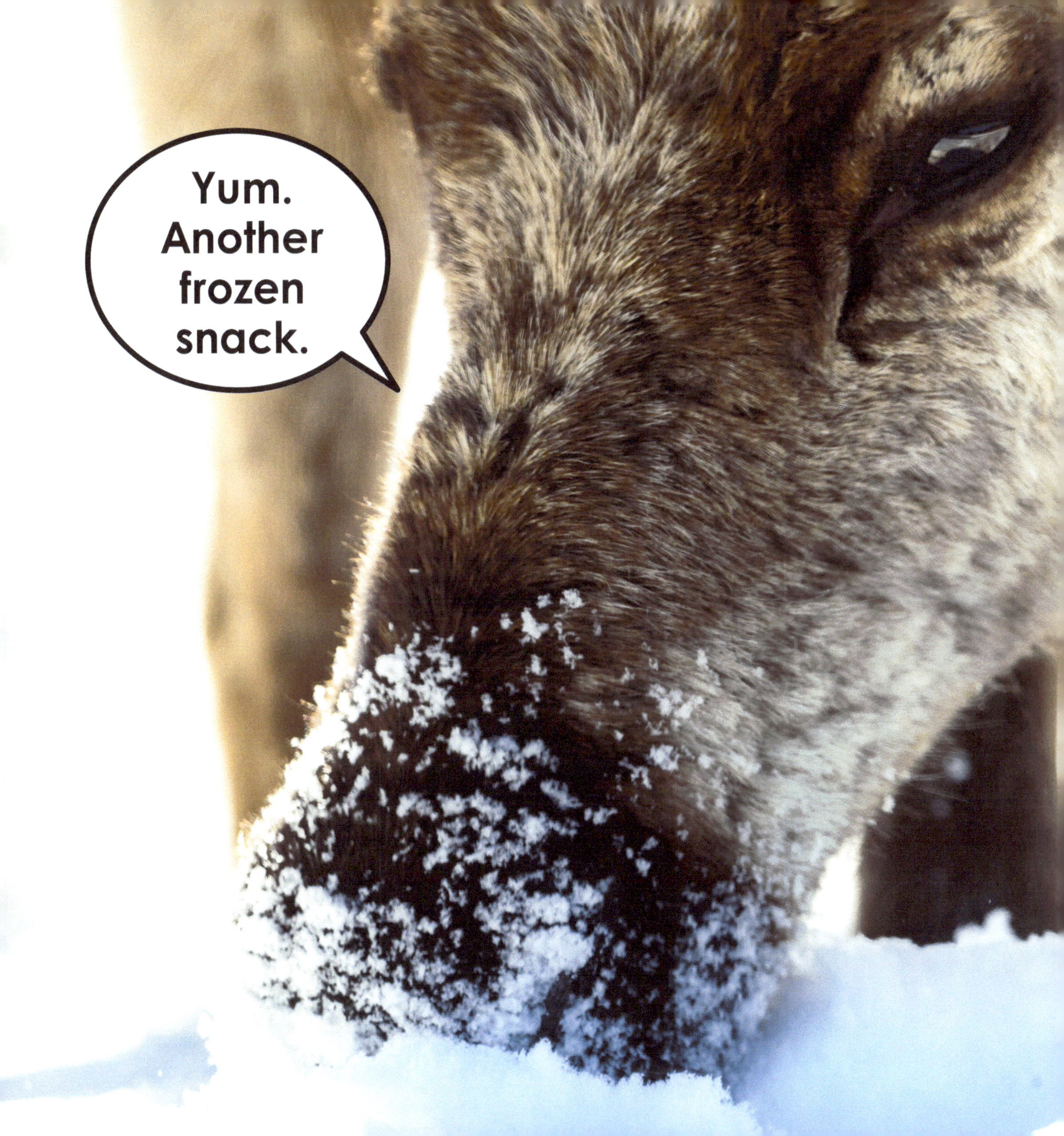
Yum. Another frozen snack.

Reindeer are "herbivores". That means they eat plants like moss, lichen, and grass.

I have a special digestive system.

Reindeer can eat foods that are toxic to other animals.

Baby reindeer are called "calves".

Calves are usually born in the spring.

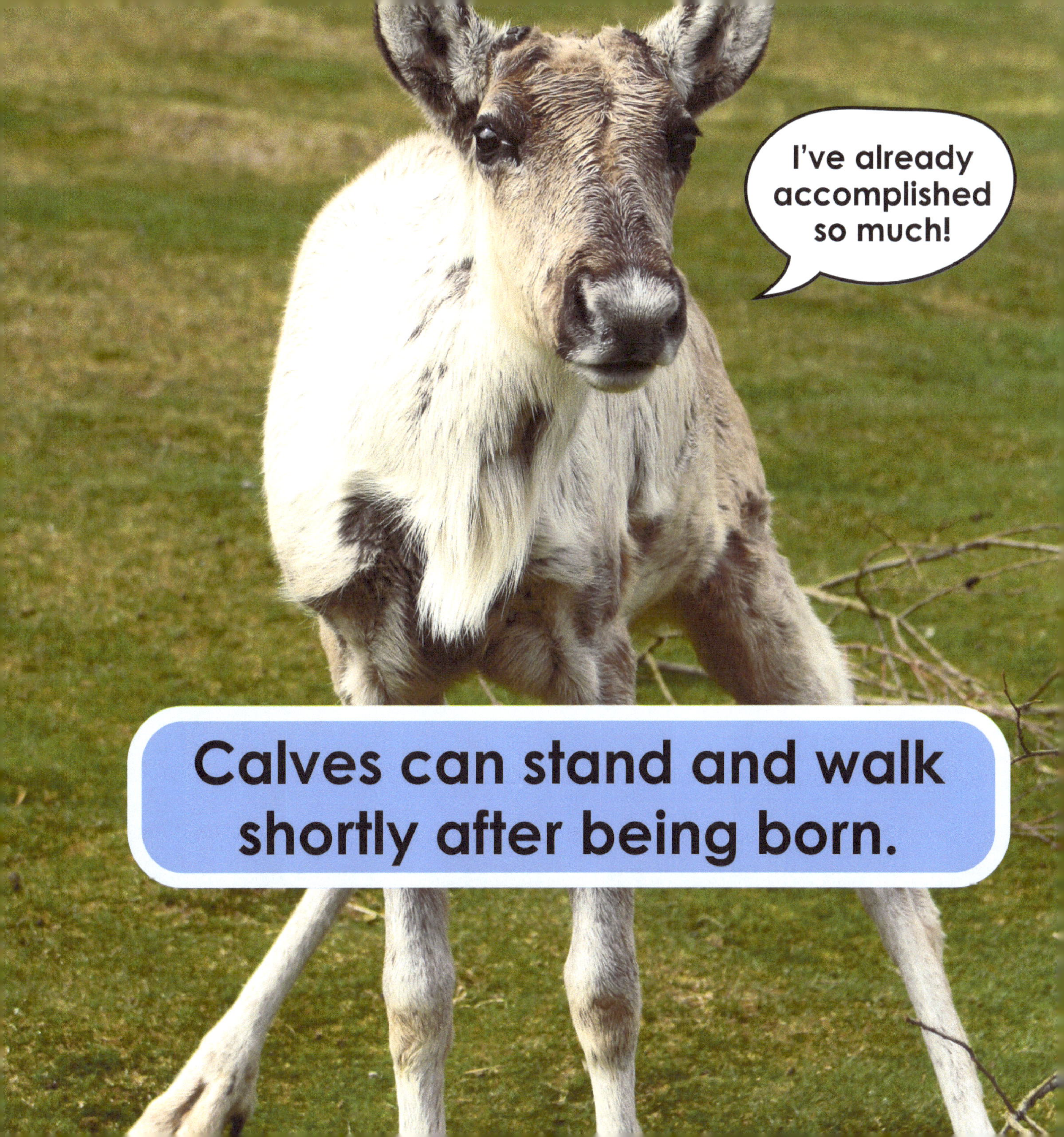

Calves can stand and walk shortly after being born.

Some reindeer are more bossy than others.

Follow me!

Reindeer herds or families have a hieriarchy.

Reindeer families like to stay together, and they even visit their relatives.

Reindeer have been domesticated by some northern peoples for thousands of years.

I am helpful to people.

They are strong and can pull sleds and carry heavy loads.

Reindeer are important to many cultures because they provide transportation and food.

In many cultures, reindeer are associated with Christmas and pulling Santa Claus's sleigh.

Hello parents!

scan here

Visit us to find out about new releases and *FREE* offers. We'll let you know when we have a new release coming out and how you can get it for FREE.
And you can cast your vote for what book we make next!

or visit here

ActiveBrainsBooks.com

---

scan here

Let us know what you think. As an independent publisher, your honest reviews mean a lot to us and our business. We'd love to hear from you!

or visit here

amazon.com/review/create-review/

FOLLOW US on Amazon.

amazon.com/author/activebrainsbooks

ActiveBrainsBooks.com

ACTIVE BRAINS

www.ingramcontent.com/pod-product-compliance
Lightning Source LLC
Chambersburg PA
CBHW060844270326
41933CB00003B/191